AMERICAN
DANCE
PORTFOLIO

AMERICAN

FOREWORD BY WALTER TERRY

DANCE PORTFOLIO

PHOTOGRAPHS BY JACK MITCHELL

DODD, MEAD & COMPANY   NEW YORK

Library of Congress Catalog Card Number: 64-11600
Printed in the United States of America
by Connecticut Printers, Inc., Hartford

For my Mother
and the Memory
of my Father

ACKNOWLEDGMENTS

I am grateful to Ted Shawn, who is not only the Father of American Dance but also the father of my career in dance photography. He introduced me to Dance by inviting me to spend a summer at Jacob's Pillow Dance Festival photographing some of the world's foremost dancers.

Lydia Joel, Editor of *Dance Magazine*, helped guide my development by her high graphic standards. I am grateful to her and to Donald Duncan, Editor of *Ballroom Dance Magazine*, for assignments which subsequently produced material for this book.

My thanks go to Lucia Chase, Co-Director of American Ballet Theatre, for permission to use photographs taken for the Company; and to Charles Payne, Associate Director of American Ballet Theatre, for permission to reprint pictures from the Company's 1961-62 and 1962-63 Souvenir Program Books.

I am most grateful to Robert Pavlik, my associate and friend, who not only suggested this book, but assisted at every stage of its progress, from the taking of many of the pictures to the page lay-out.

JACK MITCHELL
New York City, N. Y.

CONTENTS

THEATRE DANCE
BALLET II

FOREWORD

The photographer is concerned with focus but so also is the dancer. For the dancer invites the viewer to focus his interest and attention upon that part of the body which, in an instant of action, possesses the chief characteristic of a given movement. The characteristic varies with the instant: perhaps it is the brilliant beating of legs high in air as the danseur executes a grand cabriole; it might be the lyrical lift of the ballerina's rounded arms; it could well be the lascivious twist of the hip as a beatnik contemptuously flicks the world aside, or the tilt of a lovely head or even the flash of a roguish eye (there are, you know, dancing eyes) or a bare, muscled torso rippling into a contraction which may mirror anything from animal alertness to an emotional spasm.

In the theater, one *sees* the dancer's whole body but one *looks* at the ever-shifting centers of interest, at the characteristics of myriads of movements.

The special attribute of Jack Mitchell's photography is that his camera's focus and the movement focus of the dancer meet in flawless accord. Here indeed is not only a record of a body but a revelation of the center, the characteristic, the mood, the flavor of an instant of action. It is a dual portrait he gives us: a portrait of a dancer and, even more important, the portrait of that movement which truly represents the dancer's moment of life within the design of his art.

Dancers differ each from the other. That is why it is possible to see such classics as "Swan Lake" or "Giselle" over and over again, for each ballerina reveals different facets of a role. As the Queen of the Swans, for example, one ballerina might give accent to the regal aspect of the role; another, to the woman; another, to the enchanted bird. One would stress dazzling pirouettes; another, sustained balances; one, speed; the other, adagio. Not one of a batterie of ballerinas would change the choreography; only the accents, only the aspects, only the insights.

Photographers are the same. They view the dancer's body, but each sees that body in a different way. Some, with the right of artistic license, distort the dancer's body to create a subject for the art of photography. Some, with equal right and much kindness, glamorize a dancer. Jack Mitchell, however, is one of those artists of the camera who do not think of the dancer merely as subject matter. True, he uses distortion and he uses glamor but only if these are elements in the revelation of a dance truth, in the portrait of that magical and ephemeral instant of action which is, for that fleeting second, the art of dancing.

WALTER TERRY

INTRODUCTION

Photographing dancers is, for me, more pleasure than work. During the past six years I have had a very good time for I have devoted myself, almost exclusively, to dance photography.

Producing an exciting dance photograph requires a collaboration of the dancer and the photographer. Dancers are well prepared for this collaboration. Their training gives them an acute awareness of composition plus a body disciplined to execute almost any movement or pose. These qualities, plus willing and total cooperation, make dancers ideal photographic subjects.

This book is composed of a personal selection of my photographs of dancers. There has been no attempt to produce a complete historical record. The selection was limited only by the provisions that the subjects are known primarily as performing dancers and that they are American, or have appeared with an American dance company.

JACK MITCHELL

Ruth St. Denis performing "The Incense"
at Jacob's Pillow Dance Festival on July 4, 1961.
She created this dance for herself in 1906, soon after
she began her dancing career.

An early Ruth St. Denis dance called "The Yogi." This photograph was taken in 1956.

"White Jade," one of the most popular of numerous solo dances choreographed by Ruth St. Denis.

Ruth St. Denis, the First Lady of the American Dance.

"The Mevlevi Dervish," one of the many religious
dances created by Ted Shawn. Whirling begins
before curtain rise and continues until the curtain
is down. Symbolic of the solar system's movement
pattern, the whirling is an effort to attain union with
God. This photograph of the 1924 dance was taken
during a 1951 performance of Ted Shawn in the
Ted Shawn Theatre at Jacob's Pillow.

Ted Shawn, often called The Father
of American Dance, performed for
the camera his classic solo,
"O Brother Sun and Sister Moon:
A Study of St. Francis." Created
in 1931, this dance is still frequently
performed at the Jacob's Pillow
Dance Festival.

America's great modern dancer and choreographer,
Martha Graham, and Germany's Mary Wigman,
originator of modern dance in Europe. Picture
was taken in New York at 1958 reception honoring
Miss Wigman's visit to America after an
absence of twenty-five years.

Martha Graham rehearsing "Alcestis."

Paul Taylor, Martha Graham, and Bertram Ross in Miss Graham's "Alcestis."

Martha Graham—"Acrobats of God"

Bertram Ross and Paul Taylor in "Alcestis." This setting is one of many created for Martha Graham by Isamu Noguchi.

Robert Powell and Clive Thompson as Bull-Dancers in "Phaedra."

Martha Graham as Phaedra.

Martha Graham and Bertram Ross portray
Phaedra and Hippolytus in "Phaedra."

24

Bertram Ross, Martha Graham, and Ethel Winter in
"Phaedra." Miss Winter dances the role of Aphrodite.

Richard Kuch and Richard Gain, as Bull-Dancers, lift
Robert Cohan, portraying Theseus, in "Phaedra."

Linda Hodes in Martha Graham's "Embattled Garden."

Helen McGehee

Robert Powell and Helen McGehee in "Secular Games."

Robert Cohan

Pearl Lang and Dance Company in Miss Lang's
"Persephone," a dance in Prologue and Five Scenes,
with Time indicated as "The Seasons-time past
time present merged by allegory." Miss Lang is
a former principal dancer in the Martha Graham
Dance Company.

Merce Cunningham, avant-garde modern dancer and choreographer, was once a member of the Martha Graham Dance Company. He now heads his own company and school. Soft-spoken and gentle, he is admired by, and a friend of many of today's greatest abstract painters.

Paul Taylor—"Option."

Paul Taylor in "Fibres," wearing costume designed by Rouben Ter-Arutunian. Like Pearl Lang and Merce Cunningham, Paul Taylor left the Martha Graham Dance Company to develop his own group.

Alexandra Danilova surrounded by fans as she leaves stage door of the Metropolitan Opera House after her final appearance with the Ballet Russe de Monte Carlo. Balletomane Carmen Delgado is seen in foreground.

Alexandra Danilova in her New York apartment.

Alexandra Danilova, prima ballerina of the Ballet Russe de Monte Carlo during its greatest years, returned in 1957 to guest-star with the company for a gala season at the Metropolitan Opera House in New York. This picture was taken during curtain-calls after the ballerina's final performance with the company, May 4, 1957. The ballet was "Gaité Parisienne," with Danilova as the Glove Seller, Frederic Franklin as the Baron, and Leon Danielian as the Peruvian. The audience was standing, applauding, and cheering. One male admirer, in an effort to catch a flower thrown by the ballerina, fell into the orchestra pit.

As premier danseur of the Ballet Russe
de Monte Carlo, Frederic Franklin created
many important roles. Among them, The Baron
in "Gaîté Parisienne," and Champion Roper in
"Rodeo." In the "white ballets" he has danced the
cavalier to some of the world's greatest ballerinas.

Dame Alicia Markova sat for this portrait soon after
she formally retired from her brilliant dancing career,
and just prior to the announcement that she had
been appointed Director of the Metropolitan Opera
Ballet. It was at the Met, twenty-five years before,
that the English-born ballerina made her
American debut in "Giselle."

Nina Novak and George Zoritch of the
Ballet Russe de Monte Carlo in "Mississippi Dance,"
choreographed by Donald Saddler.

Nathalie Krassovska—"Don Quixote."

Leon Danielian—"Don Quixote."

Erik Bruhn and Nora Kaye of the American
Ballet Theatre photographed immediately after
dancing the "Paquita" pas de deux.

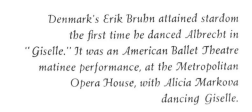

Denmark's Erik Bruhn attained stardom
the first time he danced Albrecht in
"Giselle." It was an American Ballet Theatre
matinee performance, at the Metropolitan
Opera House, with Alicia Markova
dancing Giselle.

Nora Kaye—"Lilac Garden."

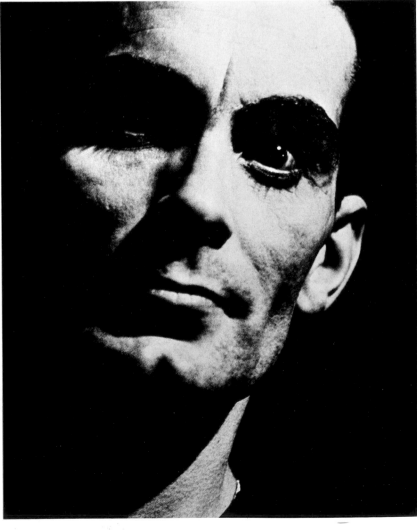

Hugh Laing

Toni Lander in American Ballet Theatre's production of "Etudes," choreographed by Harald Lander, husband of the ballerina.

Toni Lander as Odile, the Black Swan, in "Swan Lake."

Toni Lander as Odette, Queen of the Swans, in "Swan Lake."

Paul Nickel, as a child, portrayed the role of young Billy in a television production of "Billy the Kid." At eighteen he joined the American Ballet Theatre and was cast as a cowboy in the same ballet.

John Kriza as Billy in Eugene Loring's popular ballet "Billy The Kid." Mr. Kriza and other members of the American Ballet Theatre gave a particularly brilliant performance of this ballet in the East Room of the White House on May 22, 1962, for President and Mrs. John F. Kennedy and guests.

Bruce Marks left a promising career in modern dance to study ballet. At twenty-four he joined the American Ballet Theater as a principal dancer.

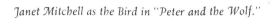

Basil Thompson as Peter in "Peter and the Wolf."

Richard Wagner as a Hunter in "Peter and the Wolf."

Ruth Ann Koesun as the Sugar Plum Fairy in "The Nutcracker."
Background painting is THE WHITE FLOWER *by Georgia O'Keeffe.*

Scott Douglas as The Bluebird in "Princess Aurora."

Gayle Young—"Princess Aurora"

Taj Selling—"Grand Pas—Glazounov"

Basil Thompson—"Princess Aurora"

Mary Gelder—"Etudes"

Kent Hatcher—"Etudes"

Lupe Serrano and Bruce Marks—"Etudes"   Lupe Serrano—"Etudes"

53

John Kriza and Ruth Ann Koesun in "Caprichos." The background painting is El Greco's VIEW OF TOLEDO.

Scott Douglas as Tancred, a Christian warrior, and Lupe Serrano as Clorinda, a pagan girl, in "The Combat."

Scott Douglas—"The Combat"

Royes Fernandez—"Grand Pas—Glazounov"

Ivan Allen—"The Nutcracker"

Sallie Wilson—"Theme and Variations"

59

Ted Kivitt—"La Fille Mal Gardée"

Elisabeth Carroll—"Les Patineurs"

Lupe Serrano—"La Fille Mal Gardée"

Sallie Wilson—"Lady From The Sea"   Glen Tetley—"Lady From The Sea"

Eleanor D'Antuono—"Miss Julie"   Rosemary Jourdan—"Miss Julie"

Bruce Marks

Scott Douglas

To avoid having one or two principal dancers perform in
every ballet on a program, ballet companies must have at
least two dancers rehearsed in any major role. This
allows an audience to see nearly all of a company's stars
on any one program. The role of Jean, the butler, in the
American Ballet Theatre's production of "Miss Julie"
has been danced by Glen Tetley, Scott Douglas, Bruce
Marks, and Erik Bruhn. The role of Julie has been
performed by Maria Tallchief, Toni Lander,
and Violette Verdy.

Toni Lander and Glen Tetley

Maria Tallchief and Erik Bruhn—"Miss Julie"

Maria Tallchief as the Swan Queen in "Swan Lake."

Maria Tallchief and Erik Bruhn—"Black Swan" pas de deux

Maria Tallchief and Erik Bruhn—"Swan Lake"

Maria Tallchief and Erik Bruhn—"Don Quixote" pas de deux

Maria Tallchief and Erik Bruhn—"Flower Festival at Genzano"

*Maria Tallchief and Erik Bruhn posed for
"Swan Lake" pictures before they performed,
or rehearsed, together in the ballet. The ballerina,
familiar with the George Balanchine choreography
for the New York City Ballet's version, spent time
between photographs demonstrating the changes
for Mr. Bruhn.*

America's leading classical ballerina, Maria Tallchief, is the great-granddaughter of an Osage Indian Chief. When an American Ballet Theatre tour took her to Miami, Fla., Miss Tallchief was made an Honorary Citizen of the Seminole Indian Tribe and granted hunting rights on their reservation.

Maria Tallchief with daughter, Elise, and husband, Henry C. Paschen, Jr.

José Limón—"Lament For Ignacio Sanchez Mejias"

72

José Limón as Macbeth.

José Limón—"Missa Brevis"

Pauline Koner, Lucas Hoving, José Limón, and Betty Jones in "Moor's Pavane." A modern dance version of Shakespeare's "Othello," it is one of Mr. Limón's greatest ballets, and among several based on classic literary works.

Ruth Currier and José Limón—"Night Spell"

Louis Falco, of the José Limón Company, as Theseus in "The Labyrinth," a ballet by Alvin Ailey.

Chester Wolenski

Gladys Bailin and Murray Louis—"Facets"

Helen Tamiris, modern dancer
and choreographer.

Louis Falco

Daniel Nagrin in Helen Tamiris'
"Arrows of Desire (Memoir #2)."

Alvin Ailey—"Hermit Song"

Alvin Ailey Dance Theatre in "Revelations,"
a dance suite choreographed by Mr. Ailey which
explores motivations and emotions of Negro
religious music. Alvin Ailey, Myrna White,
James Truitte, Ella Thompson, Minnie Marshall,
Donald Martin.

James Truitte and Minnie Marshall in "Fix Me, Jesus," one of the songs and dances in "Revelations." Alvin Ailey Dance Theatre.

"Revelations"

Bruce King

Flower Hujer as Saint Joan

Ilona Murai in Donald Saddler's modern dance version of "Winesburg, Ohio."

Donald Saddler, Maria Karnilova, Ilona Murai—"Winesburg, Ohio"

Patricia Birch in Donald Saddler's "This Property Is Condemned," a choreographed reading of the Tennessee Williams one-act play.

Norman Walker and Cora Cahan—"Clear Songs After Rain"

The Norman Walker Dance Company, made up largely of dance students from New York's High School of Performing Arts, in "Baroque Concerto." Tim Harum is featured.

Norman Walker and Dance Company in Mr. Walker's "Splendors and Obscurities."

Donald McKayle and Shelly Frankel
— "Rainbow Round My Shoulder."

Pearl Reynolds, Shelly Frankel, and Thelma Oliver in Donald McKayle's "District Storyville."

The Donald McKayle Dance Company in "Legendary Landscape." Set and costumes were designed by Normand Maxon. Japanese dancer Mariko Sanjo is in center.

Gus Solomons, Jr.

Robert Powell and Glen Tetley in
Mr. Tetley's "Birds of Sorrow."
The ballet, with costumes by Willa Kim,
is based on a Japanese Noh play.

Myra Kinch as Charles Addams-type Giselle in
"Giselle's Revenge," her modern satire of the second
act of the great classical ballet.

Glen Tetley—"Thieves' Carnival"

Carmen de Lavallade and Glen Tetley in "Carmina Burana,"
an opera in dance form choreographed by John Butler.

Kentucky-born La Meri, America's leading authority
on ethnic dance, in costume for
"The Chinese Pheasant Feather Dance."

94

Pablo Candelas

Matteo—"Natam Adinar"

*Luis Olivares and Teresa
perform in the Grand
Ballroom of New York's
Hotel Plaza for guests of
Ballroom Dance Magazine's
Ball of the Year.*

Swen Swenson, George Reeder, and Marc Breaux
as the whip dancers featured in the Broadway
production of "Destry Rides Again."

Betty Linton as The American Beauty Rose in "Flower
Garden of My Heart" production number in "Pal Joey."

Television favorites of the 1950's,
Bambi Linn and Rod Alexander.

Dancer-choreographer Peter Gennaro in his jazz
ballet, "South Rampart St. Parade," which was
performed several times on the Perry Como
television show.

Swen Swenson performs his show stopper, "I've Got Your Number," from the 1962-63 Broadway musical "Little Me."

Eleanor Powell, long-time queen of tap dancing in lavish Hollywood musical films. This picture was taken in the star's dressing room at New York's Latin Quarter when Miss Powell came out of retirement in 1961 to perform in night clubs and on television.

Grover Dale dancing Joe Layton's choreography for the Broadway musical "Greenwillow."

Harold Lang and Wisa D'Orso in a revival of "On The Town."

Marge and Gower Champion, popular dance team of motion pictures and television, dance at New York's Hotel Plaza for a Dance Magazine cover photograph.

George Balanchine, Artistic Director of the
New York City Ballet, is considered the greatest
ballet choreographer of his time. The popular
"Mr. B" is seen on stage at New York's City Center
directing dancers prior to a rehearsal of
"A Midsummer Night's Dream," his ballet based
on the Shakespeare play.

Tanaquil Le Clercq, former ballerina of the
New York City Ballet, will be remembered
for her performances in Balanchine's
"La Valse," Jerome Robbins' "Afternoon of
A Faun," and Frederick Ashton's
"Illuminations." In private life the Paris-born
ballerina is Mrs. George Balanchine.

Jacques d'Amboise, leading dancer of the New York City Ballet in Balanchine's "Apollo."

Violette Verdy and Jacques d'Amboise—"Tchaikowsky Pas de Deux"

Edward Villella—"Afternoon of a Faun"

Edward Villella

Allegra Kent

109

Conrad Ludlow, a principal dancer in the New York City Ballet, was photographed in "A Masque of Beauty and the Shepherd" while still a member of the San Francisco Ballet.

Patricia Wilde—"Gounod Symphony"

Arthur Mitchell

113

Regional ballet companies in America have prepared many young dancers for professional careers. It is notable that more and more members of professional companies have a regional ballet background. The two New York City Ballet dancers shown on this page are among a number of professionals trained in the regional Boston Ballet Company, under the direction of E. Virginia Williams.

Sara Leland

Earle Sieveling

Suzanne Farrell of the New York City Ballet was photographed while a student at The School of American Ballet.

114

Thomas Andrew, Metropolitan Opera Ballet

Charles Bennett,
Lois Bewley, and
Bill Carter, three members
of The First Chamber
Dance Quartet, in Miss
Bewley's "Pi/r²."
The ballet is a wry satire
of George Balanchine's
abstract choreography.

Marie Paquet, Françoise Martinet, Brunilda Ruiz, and Nels Jorgensen in the Robert Joffrey ballet "Pas des Déesses."

Lisa Bradley and Paul Sutherland in "Sea Shadow," a pas de deux by Gerald Arpino.

The Robert Joffrey Ballet in a practice-clothes performance of Brian MacDonald's "Time Out Of Mind." This was one of six ballets commissioned for the young company by the Rebekah Harkness Foundation in 1962. Suzanne Hammons, Nels Jorgensen lifting Lona Isakssen, Brunilda Ruiz.

Lawrence Rhodes, James De Bolt, Paul Sutherland, and Lisa Bradley in Gerald Arpino's "Partita for 4."

Lupe Serrano and Rudolf Nureyev rehearsing for a television performance.

Awaiting the arrival of rehearsal pianist Howard Barr, who was delayed at a Bolshoi Ballet rehearsal at the Metropolitan Opera House, Rudolf Nureyev utilized the time for keyboard practice.

Russian defector Rudolf Nureyev in his American stage debut at the Brooklyn Academy of Music. Appearing as a guest artist with Ruth Page's Chicago Opera Ballet he danced the "Don Quixote Pas de Deux" with ballerina Sonia Arova.

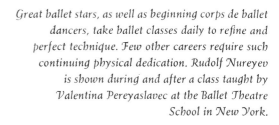

Great ballet stars, as well as beginning corps de ballet dancers, take ballet classes daily to refine and perfect technique. Few other careers require such continuing physical dedication. Rudolf Nureyev is shown during and after a class taught by Valentina Pereyaslavec at the Ballet Theatre School in New York.

INDEX

*Camera identification

A — Rolleiflex E-2, Xenotar f/3.5
B — Rolleiflex, Tessar f/3.5
C — Mamiyaflex C-2, 80mm Mamiya-Sekor f/2.8
D — Mamiyaflex C-2, 180mm Mamiya-Sekor f/4
E — 4x5 Anniversary Speed Graphic, 135mm Xenar f/4.7
F — Nikon S, 50mm Nikkor f/2
G — Nikon S, 85mm Nikkor f/2
H — Nikon F, 50mm Nikkor-S, f/1.4

40	Leon Danielian	Ballet Russe de Monte Carlo	1958	B
41	Erik Bruhn, Nora Kaye	American Ballet Theatre	1958	B
42	Nora Kaye	American Ballet Theatre	1951	B
42	Hugh Laing	American Ballet Theatre	1951	B
43	Erik Bruhn	American Ballet Theatre	1956	B
44	Toni Lander	American Ballet Theatre	1962	C
45 (2)	Toni Lander	American Ballet Theatre	1962	C
46	John Kriza	American Ballet Theatre	1961	A
47	Paul Nickel	American Ballet Theatre	1961	A
47	Bruce Marks	American Ballet Theatre	1962	C
48	Janet Mitchell	American Ballet Theatre	1961	A
48	Basil Thompson	American Ballet Theatre	1961	A
48	Richard Wagner	American Ballet Theatre	1961	A
49	Ruth Ann Koesun	American Ballet Theatre	1961	A
50	Scott Douglas	American Ballet Theatre	1962	C
50	Gayle Young	American Ballet Theatre	1962	C
51	Caj Selling	American Ballet Theatre	1961	A
51	Basil Thompson	American Ballet Theatre	1962	C
52	Lupe Serrano, Bruce Marks	American Ballet Theatre	1962	C
53	Kent Hatcher	American Ballet Theatre	1962	C
53	Lupe Serrano	American Ballet Theatre	1962	C
53	Mary Gelder	American Ballet Theatre	1962	C
54	John Kriza, Ruth Ann Koesun	American Ballet Theatre	1962	C
55	Scott Douglas, Lupe Serrano	American Ballet Theatre	1961	A
56-57	Scott Douglas	American Ballet Theatre	1961	A
58	Royes Fernandez	American Ballet Theatre	1962	C
59	Ivan Allen	American Ballet Theatre	1961	A
59	Sallie Wilson	American Ballet Theatre	1961	A
60	Ted Kivitt	American Ballet Theatre	1962	C
60	Elisabeth Carroll	American Ballet Theatre	1962	C
61	Lupe Serrano	American Ballet Theatre	1962	C
62	Sallie Wilson	American Ballet Theatre	1961	A
62	Glen Tetley	American Ballet Theatre	1961	A
63	Eleanor D'Antuono	American Ballet Theatre	1961	A
63	Rosemary Jourdan	American Ballet Theatre	1961	A
64	Bruce Marks	American Ballet Theatre	1962	C
65	Scott Douglas	American Ballet Theatre	1962	C
65	Toni Lander, Glen Tetley	American Ballet Theatre	1961	A
66	Erik Bruhn, Maria Tallchief	American Ballet Theatre	1961	A
67	Maria Tallchief	New York City Ballet	1960	B
68	Maria Tallchief, Erik Bruhn	New York City Ballet	1960	B
69	Maria Tallchief, Erik Bruhn	American Ballet Theatre	1961	A
70	Maria Tallchief, Erik Bruhn	New York City Ballet	1960	B
71	Maria Tallchief, Erik Bruhn	American Ballet Theatre	1961	A
72	Maria Tallchief and Seminole Indians	American Ballet Theatre	1961	A
72	Maria Tallchief and family	American Ballet Theatre	1961	A
73	José Limón	José Limón Dance Company	1950	B
74	José Limón	José Limón Dance Company	1960	B
75	José Limón	José Limón Dance Company	1958	B

76	Pauline Koner, Lucas Hoving, José Limón, Betty Jones	José Limón Dance Company	1951	B
76	Ruth Currier, José Limón	José Limón Dance Company	1962	F
77	Chester Wolenski	José Limón Dance Company	1963	C
77	Louis Falco	José Limón Dance Company	1963	C
78	Louis Falco	José Limón Dance Company	1962	D
79	Gladys Bailin, Murray Louis	Murray Louis and Company	1962	C
79	Helen Tamiris	Tamiris-Nagrin Dance Company	1963	C
79	Daniel Nagrin	Tamiris-Nagrin Dance Company	1963	C
80	Alvin Ailey	Alvin Ailey Dance Theatre	1961	C
81	Ailey dancers	Alvin Ailey Dance Theatre	1961	C
82	James Truitte, Minnie Marshall	Alvin Ailey Dance Theatre	1961	C
82	Ailey dancers	Alvin Ailey Dance Theatre	1961	C
83	Bruce King	Independent	1960	B
83	Flower Hujer	Independent	1963	C
84	Ilona Murai	Donald Saddler Dance Company	1958	B
84	Donald Saddler, Maria Karnilova, Ilona Murai	Donald Saddler Dance Company	1958	B
85	Patricia Birch	Donald Saddler Dance Company	1958	B
86	Norman Walker, Cora Cahan	Norman Walker and Dance Company	1963	C
87	Tim Harum, Norman Walker dancers	Norman Walker and Dance Company	1961	F
87	Norman Walker	Norman Walker and Dance Company	1961	F
88	Donald McKayle, Shelly Frankel	Donald McKayle Dance Company	1962	C
88	Pearl Reynolds Shelly Frankel, Thelma Oliver	Donald McKayle Dance Company	1962	C
89	Mariko Sanjo, McKayle dancers	Donald McKayle Dance Company	1962	C
89	Gus Solomons, Jr.	Donald McKayle Dance Company	1962	C
90	Myra Kinch	Myra Kinch and Dance Company	1953	B
91	Robert Powell, Glen Tetley	Glen Tetley and Dance Company	1962	C
91	Glen Tetley	"Play Of The Week" TV series	1960	B
92	Carmen de Lavallade, Glen Tetley	New York City Opera	1959	B
93	La Meri	Independent	1959	B
94	Pablo Candelas	Ballet Español, Ximinez-Vargas	1962	C
95	Luis Olivares, Teresa	Independent	1963	H
95	Matteo	Goya and Matteo	1963	C
96	Swen Swenson, George Reeder, Marc Breaux	"Destry Rides Again" company	1960	B
97	Betty Linton	City Center Light Opera Co.	1963	C
98	Bambi Linn, Rod Alexander	Independent	1958	B
99	Peter Gennaro	"Perry Como Show" NBC-TV	1961	A
100-101	Swen Swenson	"Little Me" company	1963	C
102	Eleanor Powell	Independent	1961	A
102	Grover Dale	"Greenwillow" company	1960	B
103	Marge and Gower Champion	Independent	1958	B
103	Harold Lang, Wisa D'Orso	"On The Town" company	1959	B

104	George Balanchine	New York City Ballet	1962	C
105	Tanaquil Le Clercq	New York City Ballet	1951	B
106	Jacques d'Amboise	New York City Ballet	1961	A
107	Violette Verdy, Jacques d'Amboise	New York City Ballet	1961	A
108	Edward Villella	New York City Ballet	1960	A
109	Edward Villella	New York City Ballet	1960	A
109	Allegra Kent	New York City Ballet	1961	A
110	Melissa Hayden	New York City Ballet	1951	B
111	Conrad Ludlow	San Francisco Ballet	1956	B
112	Patricia Wilde	New York City Ballet	1963	A
113	Arthur Mitchell	New York City Ballet	1963	C
114	Sara Leland	New York City Ballet	1963	C
114	Earle Sieveling	New York City Ballet	1963	C
115	Suzanne Farrell	Student, School of American Ballet	1961	A
116	Charles Bennett, Lois Bewley, Bill Carter	First Chamber Dance Quartet	1961	A
116	Thomas Andrew	Metropolitan Opera Ballet	1958	B
117	Marie Paquet, Françoise Martinet, Brunilda Ruiz, Nels Jorgensen	Robert Joffrey Ballet	1960	B
118	Suzanne Hammons, Nels Jorgensen, Lona Isakssen, Brunilda Ruiz	Robert Joffrey Ballet	1962	F
118	Lawrence Rhodes, James De Bolt, Paul Sutherland, Lisa Bradley	Robert Joffrey Ballet	1961	F
119	Lisa Bradley, Paul Sutherland	Robert Joffrey Ballet	1962	C
120	Rudolf Nureyev	Chicago Opera Ballet	1962	F
121	Lupe Serrano, Rudolf Nureyev	"Bell Telephone Hour," NBC-TV	1962	C
121	Rudolf Nureyev	"Bell Telephone Hour," NBC-TV	1962	F
122-123	Rudolf Nureyev	Independent	1962	F

ALPHABETICAL INDEX